Invisible Zoos

Poems with a life of their own

Invisible Zoos

Published October 2019 by Eithon Bridge Publications,
Prestbury, Cheltenham, GL52 5SD

https://eithonbridge.com

Copies of this anthology may be purchased from the poets
or ordered by email to: eithonbridge@gmail.com

Cover photograph: Karen L. McDermott

Printed by Stroudprint, Lightpill, Stroud, GL5 3NL

Contents

Introduction

In September 2018 a group of poets met at Tŷ Newydd, Llanystumdwy in North Wales, for a residential masterclass entitled *Invisible Zoos,* tutored by David Morley and Pascale Petit. We were promised the opportunity to "track and capture our poems as though they were creatures which *had a life of their own*" and we were encouraged to "bring a passion for nature, poetry and the outdoors". The poets readily accepted the challenge, keen to explore the "teeming Tŷ Newydd gardens with their vistas of the sea and distant mountains ... the wooded banks of the nearby river ... the estuary and beyond".

The course comprised workshops and periods of writing, taking full advantage of the countryside and wildlife in this inspiring part of Llŷn (the Lleyn Peninsula), including walks along the River Dwyfor, beloved of David Lloyd-George, whose grave is located nearby. A memorable exercise in *negative capability* was conducted during a walk along the coast, close to the Dwyfor estuary, where the poets observed and listened intently, aspiring to that state of mind described by Keats, in which a person "is capable of being in uncertainties, mysteries, doubts, without any irritable reaching after fact and reason". Myth, mystery and magic hovered around all week, and a number of 'daemon poems' consequently feature in this anthology.

While many of the poems here were inspired by observations and experiences during field trips, they also – naturally – reflect the varied interests of the individual poets, and their responses to the workshops attended and reading undertaken during the week and subsequently. A wide range of fauna and flora came to the fore during the course, brought to even closer focus by a variety of approaches and equipment for fieldwork, including binoculars, hand lenses, microscopes and bat detectors – many of these generously loaned by David Morley. Poets also made full use of the excellent library at Tŷ Newydd, as well as a number of inspiring books brought on the course by the tutors, including the first rate *Animal* series published by Reaktion Books and a wealth of animal myths, particularly those shared by Pascale Petit. The rich and varied course material prepared by both Pascale and David for use in workshops, and their insightful one-to-one sessions during the course, were of inestimable value to poets attending the masterclass.

By the end of the residential, we had, as promised, "created a poetic open zoo, written during fieldwork, workshops, individual tuition, and with the aid of inspiring wildlife poems". We hope readers of this *Invisible Zoos* anthology will enjoy reading a selection of the poems by a dozen poets from the masterclass, as much as we did 'tracking them down' and 'capturing them' in print.

Sharon Larkin and Simon Williams

Laboni Islam

An Animal in a Two-Piece Shell
*found in Seashells: Bivalves of the British and Northern European
Seas, by J. Møller Christensen, revised and adapted by S. Peter Dance;
words added*

Your shell may grow rapidly,
one half
a mirror image of the other.

Bury your hinge
and mantle in seabed, or
move between tide marks.

Live out your brief life
unseen, undisturbed, unsuspected
by the casual observer.

When you die,
your shape and ornament
will wash ashore

and the living
will consider the history
of the once-living organism,

the nomenclature
of your body.

Sharon Larkin

The Collector I

She dons baseball cap and jeans,
pursues the first orange tip of spring
supping at the lady's smock.

Hear her swear like a squaddie
at the seldom-settling brimstones,
depriving her of a shot.

Later, she sneaks like a peeping Tom,
to spy over a neighbour's fence
when buddleia's at its shameless best,

pulling butterflies from miles around.
Tortoiseshell, peacock, painted lady –
each one excites her; she is not fussy.

Sharon Larkin

The Collector II

In former times she might have been a man
dressed in heavy tweeds and leather boots,
bent on decimating populations
with eager sweeps of a butterfly net,
to scoop up coppers and skippers
into killing jars, spiked with cyanide.

It was the hobby of rural parsons,
their studies lined with dead Lepidoptera,
mounted, framed, labelled in Latin,
or laid to rest in glass sarcophagi –
moments hushed in polished mahogany.

Or it was a mission between wars
for famous names in pith helmets, long shorts,
swatting after monarchs and swallowtails
along the hedgerows of a foreign field:
an expeditionary force intent
on bringing dead emperors back to Blighty.

Or it was the quest of umpteen uncles:
boy scouts, arms a-boast with badges,
swishing muslin over nettles and comfrey,
dashing back to the hut with an I-spy book
to argue over arguses and female blues.

Painstakingly impaled, expertly curated,
their collections might be with us still,
except for the mites that invaded,
nibbling magnificent wings to dust,
leaving grey smudges, pointless pins.

Sharon Larkin

The Collector III

Blame John Fowles in '63
for connecting collecting with psychiatry:
Miranda Grey, chemically coshed,
became Fred Clegg's latest prey,
banged up in his cellar.
Between the three of them,
they did collecting in.

To snaffle a red admiral had seemed
to young innocents, something heroic.
Armand and Michaela Denis on safari
or the burbling Jacques Cousteau
appeared to thrill more than today's
earnest conservators,
incorrigibly knowledgeable.

Now a voyeur on autofocus
motor-drives to capture every pixel,
zooming in on velvety wings
for high scores in the Big Butterfly Count,
a cheat with technology,
cropping, applying garish filters,
plotting dots on maps on apps.

Derek Littlewood

The Bee Call

Annie stepped naked into her garden.
Smeared herself with honey, except for back, face and arms.

She addressed the hive, crooning in a low tone.
She clasped to her throat a protecting flower,

its petals pink and white. Gossamer wings quicken.
From the skep emerged a sinuous tawny stream:

a dress of honey bees, tiger-striped roiled about her.
The air swarmed in harmony. Annie was perfectly calm.

Derek Littlewood

Stranded

Seafarer! Sea fretted bladder wrack shirt, robust, branched olive
brown strap-like fronds.
Each strap with numerous air bladders in pairs, which act as floats.
Leathery marine with a strong hold-fast for a cable.
Green saline when fresh from the waves drying to a rufus chestnut
on my shoulders.
A sea belt cinches the waist of the vessel.
Murlins at my collar. Fringed with colourless jelly-like hairs.
All to the accompaniment of fife and drum
with a boatswain's pipe to welcome you aboard.
Thong-weed beneath and sea oak for leggings.
My sea bootlaces tangle from my sea boots.
All furbelows now with carragheen cuffs and a pepper dulse collar.
I'm a fine cockscomb in my red rags. I'm bladder wracked.
I'm knotted wrack, too tough to pop between fingers.
My rough stalks produce foothold for other seaweeds.
A waft of ozone drifts about me.

Derek Littlewood

Boudica and the Hare

You Mother were as shy as the hare, your hands shook
with tremor. You were as brave as Boudica at the last.

Our Queen let slip a hare from the folds of her plaid
before the field of battle. It flew left from her war chariot,

then froze, at last jinked off to the right.
Turning her head, her gold torc flashing in the sun:

Let us show the Romans they are hares and foxes
trying to rule dogs and wolves.

Our hare escaped that day, but Boudica did not.
The oracle spoke with double tongue, always uncertainly.

Ravaged by Parkinson's you left me trembling in the form,
but nourished by your rich milk to make my twisting way.

Karen L. McDermott

House of Ancient Feet

naked in your dark ruined rooms
body tattooed with sepia   the familiar
yet unloved symbols ever present

you might lean toward something else
wish yourself other   a charmed
being in a cloud of white magnolia

transported upon a tamed and noble
animal   stepping carefully through
delicate perfume   perhaps

there is even a small bird
in your fine hands   gift of ease
of gentility

confronted with what you are not
you will stand your ground
remember the woman who bore you

stoic into a battling world
the story fierce   from a womb
of many secrets you were born

to the tribe of rough fur
the wound and scar of a mother bear
whose name you do not speak

your house is solitude   its roots earthy
ancient from which you will not escape
though you walk   though you wander

sacred carrier of memory   woman
of courage you cannot recall
but I know   once you ran

wild-footed in virgin forests
gamboled through tall grasses
a digger of holes

you fed on honey
in the pink-tongued time
the long carefree months of light

Karen L. McDermott

Bodice

I dream I am marrying
for the second time
an older wiser bride

    you know of course
    I say with a wry smile
    I am no spring flower
    he says   of course

my dress will not be white   rather
light gray silk with a sheer slip
no under-garment required   the bodice
fits perfectly   a rich earthy sienna
intricately worked with smocking
tiny pearls in all the little tufts

I am walking down the aisle
when I feel something give
way   with each breath
the giving-way grows   I
am growing   taller   thicker

the bodice seems to be breaking
apart   rough and scratchy
and fragile all at once   a kind
of thin bark splitting open
in lacy lines until it peels away
drops off   reveals

the trunk of a tree   me
my bark-less torso smooth
elegant breasts elaborate
beautiful knots   exposed

in this way I choose to go on
to not hide myself   rather to accept
this tree-nature   to marry
in full honesty   I turn eyes wide
to my new love   grinning he offers
his feathering hands

Karen L. McDermott

Myth

the flowers from the north
had their mouths open
and if touched
they laughed   ignored
they closed up with a sigh

those southern flowers
seductive   sultry petals apart
they bowed down
worldly   but wary
in the heat

sea lilies fanned the water
smiled shyly   thistle
the entry point of light
stretched up into
the sky

flowers from the east
from the west   we retreated
like oysters   head and feet
in the shell consumed
by what you thought I said

what I felt you thought
and before long we did not
laugh much   did not dance
lived a ho-hum life
too stressed to notice

Caroline Messenger

Ritawika the Ring-tailed Winged Cat

I have been sent by eagle brothers
from highest mountain, deepest canyon
to enfold you in down feathers
then transform to feline griffon
padding on paws of velvet
to circle you in protection
to cushion your troubled spirit
as you stroke the uncut pinion
of my closed fan of wings.
Gradually as you look deep
into my almond topaz eyes
realisation, you can succeed.

Never ignore my ring-tailed self
these folded feathers are for flight.

Caroline Messenger

Feather on my Pillow

I lie naked on the back
of my snowy owl as it quarters
the expanse of white tundra.
He has given me the claws
of owls that will build
my soul a stairway to heaven.

Suspended aloft from the pack
barely visible in churning snow
flash of red blood-hungry tongues
heads tip back, howls echo
in empty snowscape, wolf eyes
scour the sky as dusk approaches.

My white owl makes no sound
flying on baffled, fringed wings
towards the mountain ledge
where in an open nest of twigs
lined with down I am left
to interlock claws for climbing.

Caroline Messenger

Navaho Deer Walking

Treading barefoot through cotton woods
scent of green pushes up through
pictograms in ochre canyon
toes feel into the warmth
of cloven elk prints.
Pre-sunrise and another world
imbibed through feet.

Marion New

Fox

I wear foxglove shoes
a gift from the fairies.
The flowers soften the sound
of entering a hen house.

I should tell you I'm not a good pet.

There are many like me
worn around a shoulder.
with dead, glass, eyes.
only stripped bodies left.

Aristotle said we were incomplete
because we burrow in earth.

We can only become whole
when we are licked into shape.
Do hounds lick a fox?

We teach our young
to hunt and kill.

In moonlight I ignite my tail
and assume the human form.

Marion New

Cat Chaser

With a luxuriant dark tabby coat
her mews meet the tip of her tongue.

We sing the cat's chorus.
Duetto Buffo di due gatti

Miaow, miaow,
miaow, miaow.

She walks by my side.
Will she leave

as quickly as she came?
She stalks me, haunts me

sits by my writing hand.
Mouths words on my fingers

toughens them with her tongue.
I will need to turn my head away

when she has slain
a mouse or bird.

When we sing our duet
our soprano voices mingle.

Miaow, miaow,
Miaow, miaow.

Marion New

Cloud

I'm unable to grasp this cloud
my fist would thrust through it.
I can't grip cold water.

It stands out against a stage set
of blue sky, tastes
and smells of earthy water.

Not all clouds bear rain.
This one has a grey coating.
It turns the air chilly covering the sun.

I expect it to move swiftly. The wind
flicks my hair, plays with my ears.
The water is ruffled.

New clouds hover over old mountains.
My cloud is absolutely still.

Lesley Sharpe

Second Sight

A waterfall is a blank slate
beginning again and again,
always in the midst of itself
– no time for thought
or the complications of hunger.

An eye is a self-contained world,
knows how the path winds
at the end of the garden, feels
the latch of its cold gate, how it opens
and closes, knows a bud will relax
its grip, that the wind coils
under leaves like a snail.

Lesley Sharpe

Lady Fern

Rather thin, I am pinkish when exposed,
   bluish green when mature –
my petiole long as my blade.
   I seek damp woods and stream ditches.
Even though I die down in autumn,
   my name reverberates
         Athyrium filix-femina
and as far as the reach of north rock and gully
   I echo through the late snow, make
each leaf a seasoned miniature of myself.

Lesley Sharpe

Riddle
after the Anglo Saxon

My world is made of a hundred pieces   is made of stone
I am fox, I am eel   I am two sides of a leaf
I am the rope in the current   I pull out the leaping foam
I cannot answer your question   but you must come with me
I am breathless with speed   I am a trailing branch
I slip through each crack   drink a tortoiseshell pool
I am a flat shadow   a gnat pulling water with puny legs
I am the riverbank   without me there is no rest
birdsong, or Bach   I am the dryad's grief
the cello a woodland   a clearing, the low edge of the sun
my berries are tight and sour   I rummage through shrivelled leaves
bring myself to my brackish edge   I taste salt in quartz
my word an old shell   a fossil split from sand, a strange oyster.

Theresa Sowerby

River
By the Waters of Irwell

Under bridges, footsteps, traffic, trains,
you quicken – upstream, jacksharps, roach and perch.
In soot-black walls a stubborn renaissance

of thwart shrubs roots and nestles. Branches reach,
shadows caught in water's shivering mirror.
Hugh Miller's *hapless river* lives, grows rich.

Your pulses, throbbing, shrug off sorrow;
renewed, released, you breathe and move again.
Upstream heron, mute swan, kingfisher

live, feed and breed. Each evening keening strings
of midges rise and fall. Your unstopped voice
takes up its song which, coursing over stones,

once thrilled through salmon leaping in the race
back to their natal stream; to wolf and hare;
to beech and alder imaged in your surface.

Sense-language – liquid syllables from before
Domesday, Bible, Bede and witnessed belief –
speaks. Shale, gritstone, rock, curling drifts of air

in colloquy with grasses, flowers, leaves,
become attentive – one receiving ear
tuned to a syntax of pre-conscious lives.

When crack and shift of melting glacier
rebirth microbial Adam, sculpt plastic
banks of boulder clay, thrust first fingers

of green from a chance-flung seed, your music
begins calling, conjures fragile peace
between heat and cold, cajoling back

creation. *Here is a new garden, a place*
still moulding, shaping dip and swell
under the sculptor's hand, wind and water's grace.

Held in suspension, a prelapsarian soul,
pre-conquest, pre-conscious watered valley –
Before Saxons settled, claimed your heft and roll,
named you their place of white water – Erewele.

Theresa Sowerby

The Coat

I would make you a coat of green. Oak, beech, sycamore, ash.
I would overlay leaf upon leaf like feathers on a hawk,
plait sleeves of couch grass and timothy,
weave a collar of lavender to sweeten your air.

I would pierce a pine needle, thread it with mare's tail,
sew in a lining of lichen and moss cool against your skin.
And when swallows gathered and the leaves grew ragged,
you would blaze bronze and yellow.

In the lining I would have stitched the bone of a hare
to keep you here.

Theresa Sowerby

On Her Blindness

Here building is excavation. Splayed feet
make heavy weather of rowing through earth.
I shovel, a collier shrugging soil heaps,
stereo-sniff out beetles, feel their steel
shells crack. In drought-hardened ground, food is scarce.
Sightless, I'm led by the nose. Cut off hose,
tube of a snout. Stop, twitch, switch direction,
alert to thrushes drumming up worms.

Soil crumbles from the beetle's shell. I crunch.
My wrestler's shoulders muscle through tunnels.
Earth shivers me, blood pulses opened walls.
I thrill to the thrum of rain, steady, sweet,
soaking through roots. You note my black fur,
flesh-pink hands. I know nothing of mirrors.

Susan Taylor

Aztec Love Song

I am bent double with the weight of them,
these plants I have uprooted because I would not cut them,
these bright suns, these star signs, these marigolds.
I carry them to your house and dump them
where they burn like a fire on your threshold.

They were heavy as a sack of barley.
You choose what you will do with them.
I'm finished in giving them over.

Do what you like with my love.
Plant it to spring around the paths you tread.
Leave it to wilt if you must.
These tapers I cast around your feet
rise up in a sweet musk, smoking pollen.

Susan Taylor

Ink Caps

This ancient race of organics
with tops like treetops
visibly wavers in wind.
Water is burning them.

I tap the top of one:
structure shudders,
breasts on stems,
bells ringing in downpour.

Old bodies go tarry and charred
then they vanish,
but their stalks hold firm,
perpendicular.

Who gave them the magic
to make themselves into ink?
Was it the fairy rain-bathers
melting as life melts?

Susan Taylor

Your Daemon Here

You cannot live without my element
any more than I can live without yours

Think of your life as a two-sided thing
with an upper and under way of being

I am your beneath
your belly   your breathing

You can be my mantle
                        my magic
but mostly I fear
                        my mortal foe

Drawn to your complexities
I see you have become multifold
more than the octopus

You have grown finite
     frantic
forgetting the infinite we inhabit

Gaze out over the sparkle
                              the spindrift
the long plain song of the open sea

It made you
                    made me
made us made for each other

In this very moment
I call you back
Swim with me
Swim with me

Joy Wassell Timms

Poem Hunting

A white feather drifts
into her butterfly net –

she's out to catch moths
or beetles or flies;

to inspect hairs on their wings,
the wriggle of legs,
the green black sheen

on the rounded curve
of their abdomens.

A white feather
drops into her butterfly net –

she shakes it out.

Joy Wassell Timms

The Inner Ocean
after a painting by Christine Schloe

A sea lives in her
crash-splashes through
cracks in her eyes.

A sea lives in her.
She wears a dress of salt blue,
fears sail and return.

A sea lives in her,
salt-pan of brine,
ocean in thrall to sky.

A sea lives in her,
skin marbled with clouds,
thoughts a fierce sea,
her dreams hoist white sails.

A sea lives in her
her being is water and light;
hear crash and surge,
a last wave.

Joy Wassell Timms

Daemon

At the edge of Cabin Wood
by the chipped green gate
she waits

        like a shadow that shifts
or the note of a stonechat
hidden in heather,
a presence known, not quite seen.

"Follow" she yells,
            hind legs thump-thumping

and she's visible now
               runs this way and that
twists, swerves, reverses,
a shapeshifter of bounds and leaps.

her zig-zag I follow, breathless:
a new moon stares.

Simon Williams

Crocodilian

This morning he woke
with the head of a crocodile,
great long jaw and sly eyes,
definitely not a caiman or an alligator
as his teeth now interleaved,
where other crocodilians have overbite.
His wife and kids were indifferent,
said 'Maybe it's a reaction
to the root canal, a temporary allergy'.
He tried to drive to work
but couldn't get his new head in the car.
His nostrils pressed against the windscreen, steamed it up.

The bus driver wouldn't let him on,
said there were children upstairs
and what would their parents say?
He rang in for a sicky, citing
Sebek's Syndrome. His boss said
he'd need a doctor's note
as quoting an unlikely Egyptian god
was not in the company manual.
He's not been in since.
Instead he spends his days by the water feature
on the patio. He sits with his mouth open.
Jackdaws come to pick his teeth,
cabbage whites suck all his tears away.

Simon Williams

Decoys

I've heard three ways of attracting birds.
You can stand out in a wood with seeds
in one hand and a mobile in the other.
Look only at the phone and eventually
wild robins and tits will settle on your fingertips.

At night, in a field, suck the back of your wrist.
This sound, they say, is indistinguishable
from that of a small rabbit, dying. Owls
will come, after a lazy meal. It's advisable
to wear a thick hat, just in case.

The third involves you hanging your arse
over the back of a dinghy and farting.
The bubbles mimic the sound of common eels
arriving from the far Sargasso. It's cold
around the genitals, but Oh, the Ospreys, the Sea Eagles.

Simon Williams

Four Tŷ Newydd Clerihews

Dipper
looking chipper,
as underwater browsing
cleans the feathers, free de-lousing.

Small bug,
hugger mug
under a seedling tree.
I see you; you feel the gale of me.

Fritillary,
bit of frillery,
sails spread in the sun,
older than Dimetrodon.

Dwyfor river,
long, fat, life-quiver.
Play with Gwyneth's granite toys,
play each boulder's pink noise.

Annie Wright

How Night Was Made

after a line from Tales of the Warao, Orinoco Delta

An enormous sneeze was brewing;
the Lord of the Night shook out
his sky blue handkerchief

Aschooalotl, splotl, aschootl!

and dabbed tear-streaked eyes.

When he opened them
to his surprise
dark had escaped
covering the world in blackness.

Coyote howled, jaguar hissed,
all the birds fell to Mother Earth
for protection.

His people huddled shivering,
afraid a mighty beast
had swallowed the sun for ever.

The Lord of the Night
hung his head and wept.
Tears froze on his cheeks
and he knew what he must do.

He flung crystal tears   into emptiness

Somewhere far distant
glittering splinters of light
hang in the heavens, tiny fires
by which to navigate the night.

Annie Wright

Fan-bristled Robber Fly

Dysmachus trigonis
predator

captures other creatures
on the wing

bulging convex top of thorax
hunch-backed look

hairy
bristly

abdomen tapering
dark brownish-grey

wings   two
transparent

particularly fond of capturing
Thereva annulata

the coastal silver stiletto fly

as the prey's juices are sucked out
feeding takes some time

larger robber flies
may fall victim

cannibalism is common
widespread.

Annie Wright

Coat for Jacob

I've patched you a coat
of sparrow feathers

all dunnock browns
and this year's fluff

though you long to soar
it's not made from eagle

nor robin nor finch
the showier bunch

that gather on feeders
you daily refill

wear this coat as
a charm my spuggie

the bravest step
is next, *cariad*

and even a mother
can't stop you from falling

but find in the pocket
the scut of a hare

to remind you also
to gaze at the moon

Biographies of the Poets

Laboni Islam was born in Canada to Bangladeshi parents. Her poem 'Lunar Landing, 1966' was shortlisted for the CBC Poetry Prize (2017). Her poetry has been longlisted for the National Poetry Competition (2017) and anthologized in *The Unpublished City* (Book*hug Press, 2017), which was shortlisted for the Toronto Book Awards (2018).

Sharon Larkin has been published in poetry magazines, on-line and in anthologies (eg Cinnamon Press, Eyewear, Indigo Dreams, Zoomorphic). Her book *Interned at the Food Factory* was published by Indigo Dreams in 2019, https://www.indigodreams.co.uk/sharon-larkin/4594486683. She has an MA in Creative Writing, organizes Poetry Café Refreshed, is Chair of Cheltenham Poetry Society and is the Stanza representative for Gloucestershire. She runs Eithon Bridge Publications. https://www.eithonbridge.com   http://www.sharonlarkinjones.com

Derek Littlewood lives in Worcestershire and teaches Literature and Creative Writing at Birmingham City University. He has a poem 'Kernowek Stone' in *Second Place Rosette: Poems about Britain* edited by Emma Wright and Richard O'Brien (Emma Press, 2018). He enjoys birding at Upton Warren and bat detecting.

Karen L. McDermott is an American, resident in Europe since 1981. She is a visual artist (clay, prints/monotypes, photography) and a former teacher of children's theatre. Karen retired to the south of France where she has established a writers' retreat. Her poetry often reflects the life of fields and her work has been published in the USA and Switzerland. Karen is a long-standing member of The Geneva Writers' Group and a founding member of the Leman Poetry Workshop. She won the Geneva Prize for Poetry in 2018. https://www.karenmcdermott.com   https://www.maisonenprovence.net http://www.lemanpoets.com

Caroline Messenger has been a costume designer, choreographer and mother. An Arvon course started her writing poetry and her poems have been published in the international magazine *Here/There* and an anthology *Herrings.* She now lives in rural Provence and is part of the Geneva Writers Group.

Marion New is a retired teacher who enjoyed writing with her primary class. She now has more time to write poetry, much about the natural world. She has been commended in the Manchester Cathedral Competition, awarded third place in The Sheffield Prize, published in The North and was shortlisted in the Poetry Business Pamphlet Competition 2013.

Lesley Sharpe teaches literature and creative writing in London. Most recently, her poems have been published in the *Aesthetica Creative Annual, Dragons of the Prime (*Emma Press, 2019) and *Finished Creatures #1,* shortlisted for the *London Magazine, Aesthetica* and *Bridport* prizes, and longlisted for *Primers 2* (Nine Arches Press) and Cinnamon Press 2018 Debut Collection Prize. She edits Heron for the Katherine Mansfield Society, and is a co-founder of Lodestone Poets.

Theresa Sowerby lectures and writes on a range of literary topics and runs *Real Live Poets*, a Poetry Society Stanza group based in Manchester. She has won prizes for plays and poetry, including a 2018 *Wergle Flomp* award for comic verse and has been published in several magazines and online. Her poem *Calder* has been published in the Gingko Prize 2018 Ecopoetry anthology.

Susan Taylor began writing in her teens in the idyllic setting of her family farm in the Lincolnshire Wolds – Tennyson country. An ex-shepherd, she has become rather a turncoat now, with much sympathy for the plight of the wild wolf. She has eight published poetry collections, including *Temporal Bones*, published by Oversteps Books in 2016. Susan is a keen performer of her poetry and has developed and toured many collaborative poetry shows, including *La Loba – Enchanting the Wolf* and *The Weather House*, which appeared as an Indigo Dreams Poetry Pamphlet in 2017
https://www.indigodreams.co.uk/williams-taylor/4594076848.

Joy Wassell Timms is based in Manchester and Conwy. She has an MA in Poetry from Manchester Metropolitan University and has been published in The North, Iota, Haiku Quarterly, Dream Catcher and other magazines and anthologies including Best of Manchester Poets. Shortlisted for Cinnamon Press Pamphlet Prize 2017. Joy co-runs the Manchester Stanza group. She was appointed Writer-in-Residence at Burnage Library in July 2019.

Simon Williams has eight published collections, his latest being a co-authored pamphlet with Susan Taylor, *The Weather House* https://www.indigodreams.co.uk/williams-taylor/4594076848, published in 2017 by Indigo Dreams. Simon was elected The Bard of Exeter in 2013, founded the large-format magazine, *The Broadsheet,* and produced the well-received *PLAY* Anthology. He has created the science poetry show, *Cosmic Latte.*

Annie Wright's new collection, *Dangerous Pursuit of Yellow*, came out with Smokestack Books in February 2019. Following Invisible Zoos, her obsession with pigments is shifting to an obsession with the natural world and the path of the shaman. She leads poetry workshops in Scotland and runs The Lit Room Press.

Notes on the Poems and Acknowledgements

The poets in this anthology wish to thank **David Morley, Pascale Petit** and the staff at **Tŷ Newydd** for the excellent Invisible Zoos masterclass and the wealth of inspiration imparted and information shared from books, field guides and handouts. Specific references are included below. We would also like to acknowledge the mutual inspiration and support of fellow course members.

Pages 8-10 **The Collector.** Sharon Larkin acknowledges Peter Marren's article *Wings of desire: Why the hobby of Butterfly collecting is over – it's all about conservation now* (The Independent, 10 August 2015), and '*Rainbow Dust: Three Centuries of Delight in British Butterflies*' by Peter Marren, published by Square Peg, 2015.

Page 12 **Stranded.** Derek Littlewood acknowledges *Sea Weeds* from Richard Barnes, *Coasts and Estuaries,* Hodder & Stoughton, 1979.

Page 22 **Fox.** Marion New acknowledges Martin Wallen, *Fox,* Reaktion Books, 2006.

Page 26 **Lady Fern.** Lesley Sharpe acknowledges David Streeter, *The Collins Flower Guide,* 2010.

Page 28 **River *By the Waters of Irwell*** by Theresa Sowerby is the final section of the sequence *Manc Dante* – a re-imagining of *The Divine Comedy* set in Manchester.

Page 30 **The Coat** by Theresa Sowerby has been published in the magazine *Pennine Platform.*